Forged With Fire

Mikayla Campbell

BookLeaf Publishing

India | USA | UK

To the warriors that carried me, when I was too
weak to carry myself.

ACKNOWLEDGEMENT

I would like to express special thanks and gratitude to my Mum, without whom this book would not exist. Thank you for always encouraging me to follow my dreams, no matter how crazy they may seem.

Also, thank you to Sharnee for endlessly listening to my rambles throughout the creation of this book.

From The Ashes, You Rise.

Sweetheart, delight rolls from your tongue.
Your laughter sounds like the ending to my
favourite story- happy.
I want to find all the puzzle pieces you hide
when you think I'm not looking,
If only to complete the picture, to see your
smile.

I know you haven't always felt this way.
There were days that fiends clawed at your
heart,
Their claws elongated and sharp, shredding and
wild.
There were days that you couldn't get out of bed
in the morning,
and even now there are still days like that.

But you push through it,
You take all that strength buried within your
chest,
it lines the spine that holds you upright,
coats the rib cage that protects your precious
heart, such a strong muscle.

You rise, you rise, you rise.

On the days that feel like the world has again
fallen,
and that the pain surrounding you is too much to
bear,
you take that pain and give it purpose,
and from the ashes burnt to the ground,
surrounded by stale smoke-
you, you wondrous being,

You rise.

Emergency Exits and Therapy Sessions

We are worn into the ground, like a discarded
cigarette.
Leaving tobacco on the bottom of your leather
boot-
Then expected to apologise for the stench left
behind.
It does not matter that we are burning.
That our bodies are used as emergency exits for
men with troubled pasts.

We are more than a cheap 'therapy' session,
We are more than a quick escape.
We are more than a number to dial when you are
drunk,
In hopes of picking up for the night.

You see us as numbers, body counts to add to
your list.
As objects to brag about among friends, on how
easily you opened our legs.
If one of us leaves, there will always be another
to replace the last.

We are toys that are in your hands as soon as we
leave the conveyor belt, aren't we?

You do not see our worth.
Our pride.
Our fight, or our spirit,

And in turn, we do not see it ourselves.

Haunted

7

I wish you thought of me every time your nose
bleeds,
I wish I'd left a scar above your left eyebrow that
corresponded with my right hook- but most of
all I wish that you woke at 3 am with my face in
your mind and my voice in your ears.

I wish you were haunted, the way you haunt me.

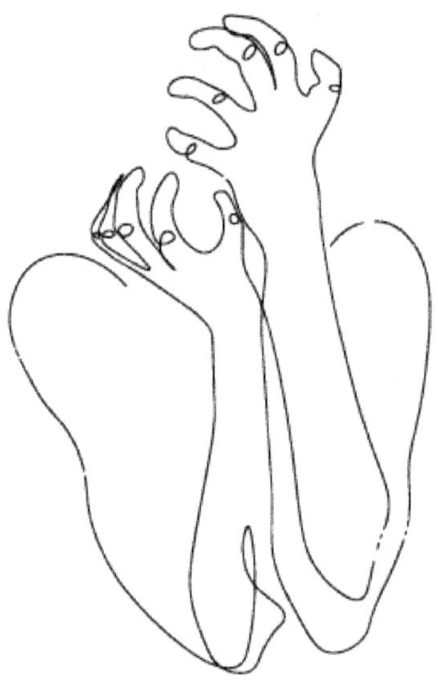

One Touch

The bruises around my wrists only remind me of
one touch.
One touch that stole millions from inside of me
and tucked them under his belt. One touch that
penetrated my insides and clawed at my heart.
One touch is all it takes for the gnashing and
grinding to start in my gut.
One touch is all it takes to send my heart into
overdrive.
One touch is all it takes to send me back to that
place three years ago.

Three years it has been, and I'm still afraid.
I promised myself at sixteen that I was done
being afraid anymore.

Red Wax

Red wax drips down the walls,
Not blood. Not blood.
Home is where the heart is right?
Why is mine splattered throughout this
structure?
Holes line the walls,
Where a once angry fist left its mark.

I spend my last remaining days patching them
up.
Smoothing over the dents and crevices I'd pay to
forget.
Scars that mar the place I once called safety.
Some nightmares are never truly forgotten.

My pillow smells of bubblegum,
An innocent enough scent.
It still turns my stomach though,
After all these years.

I place a coin in the wishing well,
that consists of a broken money box.
Perhaps I should wish for a new one.
No.

I have more important things to wish for.

Don't we all?

Yes, Woman.

The shade of brown, deep like fallen bark
Spreads across my newly plumped lips.
I have grown into my rounded face and shapely
hips,
and must accentuate that which screams
'woman'.
Pulling dark opaque tights over small legs,
Yes, woman.
But not too much.

Tights catch on pricked skin, no longer flush.
Hair now growing in places where a woman
should be smooth.
Yes, woman.
But never too much.

For women do not grow hair, women do not
cuss, women are nothing but polite.
We must always be the version of woman that
society longs to see,
Smooth, thin, accentuated, well-spoken.
and even at thirteen, this I know.

Women smell of flowers, or vanilla, or
bubblegum.

Women are small, yet larger in places a woman
should be.
We are talkative, yet quiet when it comes to
'men's business'
We are walked over, like rotting doormats, again
and again.
Never noticed until you need something to wipe
your feet upon.

Even at thirteen, this I know.
Being a woman isn't all it's chalked up to be.

Creating Our Own Reality

I never knew what it was to fight back,
Not until there sparked a need.
That need has spread like a forest fire,
Enveloping all that I call safety and home.

I listen to the earth, waiting for a sign.
A sign that it too has tired of our lazy tongues
and indolent hands,
I wonder what my mother would say, or her
mother.
Would they be proud of who we have become
today?

The ground begins to shake, and with it comes
an uprising.
Change only requires an instant.
An instant to renew, an instant to die, an instant
to transpose.

We have no crystal ball, no fortune teller, no
glimpse of the future.
So taking our wounded bodies, our weary souls,
We must create our own ending.
Write our own words.

And try not to break our own hearts in the process.

I Do

I saw the ocean in her eyes,
Waves crashing, slipping up the sandbank.
"You're not supposed to love her"
Oh but I do. I do.

They are the words I want to say on our wedding
day,
Once I unlearn the prison speak of a world
where love isn't love,
It is power, money, investment.
Not a given right.

I hear thunder in her voice,
and like storm clouds she too can render the sun
hidden,
like a small child playing hide and seek.

She knows how to make something so big seem
meaningless,
like the worries that keep me up at night in
sweat-stained sheets.

And I know that when the minister asks me "Are
you sure? Do you love her?",
I will say "I am, and I do"

You Are Already Complete

"Please", she breathes the word like a prayer.
Like a final lifeline being thrown out to sea.
I watch as she searches the many faces.
within the crowd of people, she looks.

I want to tell her,
"Darling, don't seek in others what you can find
within yourself"

She searches for strength.
She searches for courage.
She searches for a missing piece, something to
complete her heavy heart.

She does not know that all she wishes for,
all that she rummages through past lovers and
heartbreaks seeking to find,
she has always had within her own steel ribcage.

Her lungs breathe spirit, her heart beats tenacity.
Her muscles pump with the ferocity of a wild
beast,
and she cannot be tamed.

Guarded Heart

Demons hide.
Under your bed, in your closet?
No.
In your heart. In your mind.

You are at war, and you are losing.
The ribbons of flesh cascade from your chest.
The smell of iron and dust fills the room.
Light flickers and screams fill the distance.

Fear is a funny thing,
It does not have to make sense, in order to
overwhelm.
To shut down the senses, and trap you within
your mind.
All you feel is your heart pounding, mind racing,
breaths become a stolen gasp.

Let it go.
Let it go, darling.
Shh. There's nothing to fight or fly from now.
Safety is within your own guarded heart.

A Poison To Be Used Just Right

Bittersweet liquid swirls in the glass,
leaving a stain where it touches.
The scent of flame and wood rising.

Take a sip, hell take a gulp—
but don't let it poison you.
Your anger is righteous,
don't let them dampen it down.

It fills your veins, replacing blood,
with something new, something bolder.

You are powerful, but know that too much
power—
in the wrong hands, leads to destruction.
Do not use your fury to destroy,
we have enough decay in our world.

Instead, use it to build.
Take that power and give it purpose.

Renew.
Evolve.
Aspire.

Create.

Silver Dagger

I am a silver dagger lying against an oak dresser,
Dangerous. Rebellious. Deadly.
Yet beautiful.

The intricate designs throughout my spine hold
me together.
Crafted through a language all but forgotten.
Forged with the blood of those before me.

I am often quick to anger,
quick to make my mark,
and leave death behind.
Uncaring of who's blood meets my hilt.

I am a silver dagger lying against an oak dresser,
Dangerous. Rebellious. Deadly.
But sometimes, sometimes I don't want to be a
harbinger.
I don't want the power that coats my tongue.

I am no goddess. No warrior. No soldier.

I am now simply a girl, a girl who recognises the
power in bloodshed,
a girl who knows that you don't need to be a
dagger, a sword, or a blade—

to leave a scar.

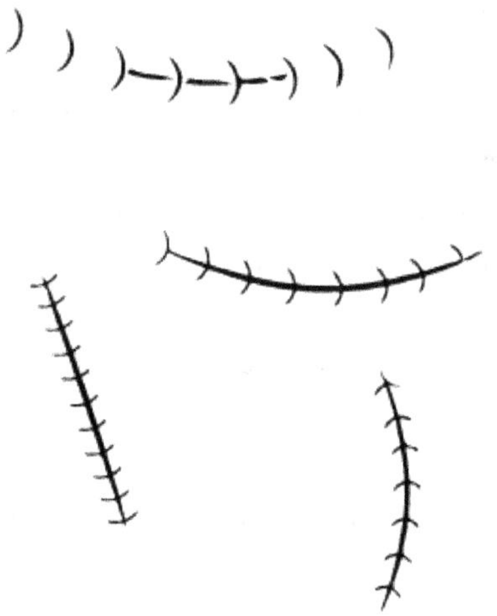

God of War

He thrives in discord.
As the God of war— it would be expected.
Never turn your back on bloodshed.
For you will soon find a knife buried within your
spine.

I didn't know that decay and destruction held a
scent.
But it is unmistakable.
The metallic scent of blood.
The indescribable scent of burnt flesh.
The familiar scent of sweat and tears fill the air.

I look to my left, carnage.
I look to my right, flames.
I look up, and it seems even the sky has tears to
shed.

War isn't coming. It is already here.
But I am the only one who can see it.

Within Four White Walls

Four white walls.
A call bell.
A bed.
Slanted doors and flat door knobs.

I smell antiseptic, and the leftover aroma of
alcohol swabs.
I hear other patients crying, they range from soft
sobs, all the way to hysterical screams.

I say a selfish prayer, that their echoes will stop
filling the halls.

Four white walls.
A call bell.
A bed.
Slanted doors and flat door knobs.

I wonder if this will be the rest of my life.
In and out, through a revolving door—
A door that doesn't open without permission.
Permission that isn't mine to give.

Nurses busy themselves, with things far more
important than care.
The fault is not theirs to carry though.

It is what it is.

The girl next door to me slides a folded note
under my door.
"They are always watching"
I wonder aloud whether she may be right.
But just because we are seen, doesn't mean we
are heard.

Four white walls.
A call bell.
A bed.
Slanted doors and flat door knobs.

I tire quickly of cold showers,
hourly checks, and medication rounds.
Watching others doped into oblivion.
Wondering if ignorance is truly bliss.

If so, I'd like a slice of it too.

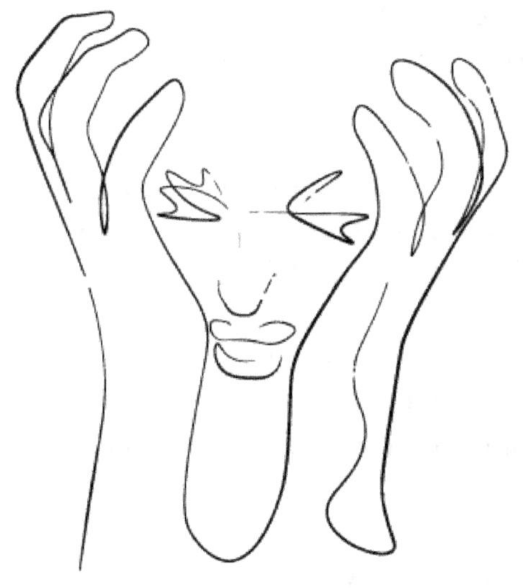

I Feel This Too

34

Dust settles on my worn keys,
and like an old piano creating a melody—
that only my ears can hear.
My fingers slowly wipe it away.

There are many ways a story can be told,
but I often think writing is the strongest.
Each reader takes home a different key,
a different passage that hits close to home.

And as I allow the words to pour out,
I wonder, if the world will ever see the beauty,
in bearing your soul on paper, with ink.

Allowing the words to bleed as I have done,
many times before.

I do not expect words to heal you,
I do not expect them to ease your pain.

But maybe, just maybe..
You'll know that you're not alone.

In this messed up, greed driven, unequal world.
In this painful and heart wrenching era.

In this place where you are surrounded by
people, but have never felt more lonely.

You have words.
To remind you that—
as long as the pen hits the paper,
as long as the pain spreads across the page,
There is guaranteed to be someone who reads it
and thinks

"wow, I feel that too"

Breathe

37

Like an iron hand, gripping my heart.
Like a worn blade, carving my flesh.
Like a tired song, haunting my mind.

This is a panic attack.

Death, decay, destruction all reign.
I feel the dust settle on my weary bones—
too afraid to lift even a finger.

As though it will upset the cosmic scale of life,
and it will be my own life I forfeit in repayment.

To bring balance once again.

Breathe, breathe, breathe.

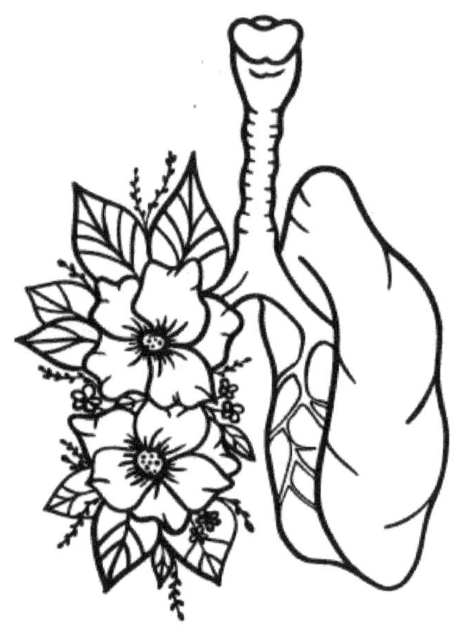

Safety

I recall too easily the nights of creeping into the
safety of my mothers bed,
with my small bear rattling along behind.
Thinking 'I'll be safe here, the bad dreams will
leave, along with their sour taste.'

Those nights continued, well into my youth.
So much to fear, and so few pockets of safety.
In such a twisted and corrupt world.

But Mum, I'm not scared anymore.

That may be the most sincere thing I've ever
written or will ever write.

I'm not afraid anymore.
I'm not afraid.

The bad dreams, night sweats, spikes of
adrenaline,
The taste that coats my mouth, screaming "You
are not enough",
The memories, the safety missing upon my
loaded gun—

They hold no power now.

For safety has always been a place within my
own heart,
It's just taken me twenty-five years to realise
that.

Shattered

41

I watch as her heart shatters,
like a wine glass hitting a cool marble floor.
There are too many pieces to count,
and I can't help but wonder how long she will
spend,
picking up each jagged piece through bleeding
fingers,
just to try and put them back together again.

To make them whole.

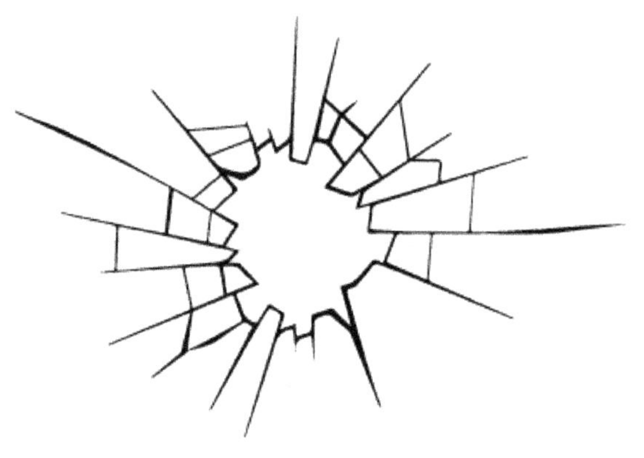

Fuck The Rules

Green eyes stare into the distance,
unseeing, yet understanding.
I know what she is thinking about.
And my heart breaks for her.

"You are not allowed to love her"
That is what they say.
And as a tear runs down her pale cheek,
I know those words are haunting.

Who are they to tell us whom we can love?
To tell us that our feelings are anything less than
holy?

Because I know, the love I feel for her could
build a steeple—
or hell, even burn one down.
Until nothing but ash remains.

I would set the world on fire, and watch it
crumble,
if only to make her smile.
Perhaps that makes me the villain in this story.

But to see the way her eyes light up, watching
the unusual colours of flame,

Well, I'm reminded that I don't want to be the
good guy.

If our love is wrong, then I don't want to be
right.
If our passion is impious, then I don't want to be
holy.

All I want is her,
and all she wants is me.

And it doesn't matter to us,
if some book tells you,
this isn't how it's meant to be.

Dancing With Death

Suffocation isn't enough to kill me,
like a drug – I've grown a tolerance to that.
I can breathe when there is no air left in the
room,
when my lungs cease to contract, and when my
heart pounds wildly.

A knife to the back isn't enough to kill me,
I have the scars to prove it; been there, done
that.
I can pull that metal dagger out with my own
two hands,
and patch up the bloody mess left behind.

You'll have to try harder.

Drowning isn't enough to kill me,
for I have grown gills over the years.
The crashing waves and salty water are friends
of mine,
and I am used to the way they pull me under to
say hello.

A noose will do you no good,
My neck already bears the mark of rope,

and I can guarantee you, I will have it torn
apart—
before we reach the gallows.

You'll need to try harder.

I will not go down without a fight,
not when I have come this far.

I spent so much time trying to end my own life,
that you will not take the gift of a second chance
away from me.
I will protect it as fiercely as I would protect my
daughter's baby laugh.

And if you know anything of what a mother
would do for her young,
You had better start learning to survive as I did.

For I guarantee the ocean, the knives, the rope
— will not be a friend to you,
as they are to me.

Know that a dance with death teaches you to
survive.

I Hope You Take This World By Storm

I hope you know,
that even though the light is hard to see,
it has always been there.

Your heart encases the brightest star,
and though one day it may go out—
your life is yours,
to live to the fullest,
to live unapologetically,
to find happiness, upon your own two feet.

And with your iron spine,
your flowerbed rib cage,
and your still breathing lungs,

I hope that you take this world by storm.

9 789357 445887